here the sun's for real

here the

autumn hill books | bloomington, indiana

sun's for real

selected poems

by josé eugenio sánchez

translated from the spanish by anna rosenwong

This is an Autumn Hill Books Book
Published by Autumn Hill Books, Inc.
1138 E. Benson Court
Bloomington, IN 47401 USA

Poems comprising this collection were first published in *physical graffiti* © 1998 by Colección Visor de Poesía, España; *la felicidad es una pistola caliente* © 2004 by Colección Visor de Poesía, España; *escenas sagradas del oriente* © 2009 by Almadía; *galaxy limited café* © 2011 by Almadía

Design and layout by Justin Angeles from a concept provided by Anna Rosenwong

ISBN: 9780998740027
Library of Congress Control Number: 2018939923

ÆB

contents

galaxy limited café

s e x i n s p a c e a n d e v e r y t h i n g i n b e t w e e n

acknowledgements

My collaborations with José Eugenio began in 2006 when he was in residence with the International Writing Program at the University of Iowa, where I had the honor to be an Arts Fellow in the literary translation MFA. To the IWP and the University of Iowa I am intensely grateful. Thanks also to the Banff International Centre for Literary Translation and to the UC Irvine's International Center for Writing and Translation, as well as the many editors who have given these translations a home in their journals.

"climax with double cheese" was published as a chapbook by Sin Papeles in 2015.

Individual poems have appeared in literary journals as follows:

the day of the guacamayas | *World Literature Today* and *Two Lines*
here the sun's for real | *World Literature Today*
czeslaw milosz gets off the train at fuengirola | *Asymptote Journal*
ray tom's daring heroes | *Asymptote Journal*
far west will never can forget | *Brooklyn Rail: InTranslation*
whorehouse raid (music by ry cooder) | *Brooklyn Rail: InTranslation*
brave men don't set foot in barber shops: sue ellen | *Brooklyn Rail: InTranslation*
ned kelly one hot morning: norma lee | *Brooklyn Rail: InTranslation*
to a nose: | *Brooklyn Rail: InTranslation*
i've got gold fever 120 degrees | *Two Lines*
dust highway | *Cartographie Curieux*
an outline for the reconstruction of events | *The Kenyon Review Online*
jeannie duval's cheek tickled by a paris fly 1852 | *The Kenyon Review Online*
helpless (and in my mind i still need a place to go | *The Kenyon Review Online*

my landladies | *The St. Petersburg Review*
© samo 6:36 | *The St. Petersburg Review*
suddenly new york | *The St. Petersburg Review*
i'll be part of it (brunch remasterized) | *Sand Journal*
hot feet cool head | *Eleven Eleven*
a true hero of the revolution | *Eleven Eleven*
how to get to montego bay (the movie) | *Eleven Eleven*
happiness is a warm gun | *qartslunni*
they speak of deep resentment | *Gulf Coast Magazine*
the incredible world of machines | *Tupelo Quarterly*
galaxy limited cafe | *Tupelo Quarterly*
video | *Brooklyn Rail:In Translation*

la felicidad es una pistola caliente

cool

happiness is a warm gun

eta killed students policemen chauffeurs nurses officials
the ira, ladies who went to buy groceries
idi amin, congress members farmers gardeners workers soldiers jockeys
child molesters parish priests
augusto killed diplomatic relations
john doe killed kennedy
the cia killed jimi hendrix al wilson jesucristo karen carpenter
janis joplin john lennon beavis & butthead
the fbi, ma baker vincent vega
tommy larrin al capone felix pappalardi
the kgb, mayakovski trotsky and bukowski
the bbc killed lady di
and mother theresa of calcuta
and the titanic's 1551 passengers
and the premier league's 17 stadiums
kraft killed heinz
pepsi, coke
coke, gringos
ddt, lice
lsd, protestants
pvc, styrofoam
al qaida, themselves
the kkk, malcolm x bob marley martin luther king garrincha and othello
jp ii killed jp i
aburto, colosio
yolanda, selena
camelia, emilo
fuenteovejuna, the commander
boredom, syd vicius
oj simpson didn't kill anybody

the police killed indigenous people in chiapas
manchester killed bayern's hopes with a last-minute goal
emi killed the beatles
the us army killed thousands of dangerous old people and children
from korea japan vietnam nicaragua panama iraq yugoslavia
and 140 in a building in oklahoma
video killed the radio star
the pri killed 1 972 545 square kilometers
the pgr killed two birds with one stone
the sep killed orthography
william burroughs, his wife

: life was invented by money

here the sun's for real (like the sun in monterrey)

the architecture is beef stew
and a carrot juts onto the macroplate

people sweat with an easy smile
in the factory some flour tacos unfurl from their aluminum wrappers
folks will line up early tomorrow
and on the corner guacharaca steel-toed boots a parabolic antenna
a hand like the manager's orders on a fat woman's bottom
dark glasses paint thinner siberia's fried tortillas
and others think they should criminalize abortion
fire the coach   dance till they drop
outlaw advertisements in puerta del sol

meanwhile
tycoons sell the hills in little bags
girls in bikinis fill the trunk with beer
celso piña plays for us
and according to stella (hostess of the parthenon)
soldiers take 12 minutes to ejaculate
waiters 3 to get to you
and millionaires in helicopters
7 to cross the city like spray paint across a wall

meditation on the shores where the tortoises bury their eggs

oh no no no:
money makes me happy yes
and I'm happy for women and men with money yes
and for the places where they have it

my weakness will be to die in mr burns's vault
in the internazionale's checkbook
in pauline c's powder compact
I adore money
I want four clones modeling outfits for me every morning
and golf commentators chatting me up at night

in these moments of love tightrope rebound jai-alai ice rink
the backseat of the car
where the only thing that matters is money
and sex for money
and for money the singer sleeps with a man who's crazy & abusive
& an agent & a degenerate: a 20th century man

these days it should be different
but there's not much i can do with this cucumber mask on
and oh god i nearly just spilled my martini

hot feet cool head

chucho deft left wing so skilled and zigzaggedy
the kind they don't make anymore
runs to the corner flag
and pisses
the official flashes him the first card of the game
chucho pisses on the ref
the back-up ref
the head inspector
the first aid kit
on the santos supporters
and the other fans go wild
chucho chucho oe oe oe
the judge demands assurances
a rival team's manager tests the piss
and faxes fifa to demand they intervene
there's talk of doping
chucho's trainer and teammates try to calm him down
and chucho pisses on the flag bearers
on the commentators photographers waterboy doctor cheerleaders
team shrink
the seven official balls won't even bounce off your ankles
the hooligans shout themselves hoarse cheering on their daring eleven
and he happily produces waterfalls against the sides
and threatens to piss on the trophy case
that belongs to the brazilian national team
and the argentinean and uruguayan and paraguayan ones too
what a night

chucho deft left wing so skilled and zigzaggedy
the kind they won't make anymore (per concacaf's recommendation)
wearing dark sunglasses like he'd missed a penalty shot
and drunk like it'd gone in
strolls on down the boulevard

dying of thirst (a song by nanker phelge)

that day we ate chickpeas with whiskas
and drank all the beers in the bodega
and chain-smoked joints till we rolled with laughter
and the sun came back up
and we bought warm superior
and when it seemed like things would come together
you asking for nails down your back or to be thrown to the floor
—I don't remember exactly—
a water stain appeared on the carpet
shyly spreading
and then buckets and buckets and buckets and night all over again
and more buckets
and the caterwauling cats like an insolent violin
and the come-down
and it's best you left through the window
and the empty fridge
dying of thirst
soaked   sneezing
I lay there dazed

the music of clattering canines

we were so poor in my house only the dog worked
he worked as a police dog

he'd leave for work early with his hat and bulletproof vest
and get back the next day with dark circles under his paws
to eat our scraps

the following morning
collar shined club oiled
heading out to headquarters again

we were very poor and lived to the letter of the law
the dog was always confiscating things
and despite the captain's orders
he wouldn't stop wagging in the face of danger
or in front of the doctors
who diagnosed him with an irredeemable loss of smell

© samo 6:36

that cloudy morning when they told john henry
(the best steel driver who ever worked on the rails)
that he was being replaced by a machine
he kept his calm
and went right on driving steel till he died

18797 thousand ties john henry
drove after that cloudy morning
:one tie more than the machine

another morning
this one in new jersey
jean michael woke with one eye closed

like a rag run over furniture
he made it to the bedroom
and humming a tune
looked for a vein

mornings like this
cloudy
when it feels like nothing will happen

the crickets sing a wind-up toy

the day that turned out to be the disaster everyone'd
warned about he didn't even notice
and hung around at the party
and later at home put on miles davis uneasy

time of shortage
in which everyone known
had scratched their pipes until they seemed like fresh chrome
a middle manager's shirt couldn't get cleaner

we're birds squeezed together on a branch

he acquired the ability
to tolerate cheerfulness from those who make life impossible
and to sometimes escape notice

we're birds fearful of being a cage

fortunately days have nights
every backside has a front
and questions have many answers

birdsong

the hinges merge into a flock
the foot of the sofa dies with each falling tree

the bathroom has no pulse neither does the sprinkler
the pupil of the toilet bowl
retains your etched image

if you had kissed one of these walls
what would have happened
if you had left your clothes behind:

the day of the guacamayas

quails dressed up as guacamayas
ostriches dressed up as guacamayas
eagles dressed up as guacamayas
toucans condors doves butterflies dressed up as guacamayas
blue-footed boobies dressed up as guacamayas
ravens pelicans sparrows mockingbirds cardinals dressed up as guacamayas
my parakeet and i dressed up as guacamayas
it was the day of the guacamayas

the little parrots dressed up as guacamayas
snub the guacamayas who didn't bother dressing up
the magpies dressed up as guacamayas were pecking at every little grain
cob and bare spot
the storks dressed up as guacamayas circled
the cows dressed up as guacamayas didn't have a clue what to do
it was the day of the guacamayas

my parakeet is a flock of beauty
and some big nasty birds dressed up as guacamayas
knit their brows when we came into view

but one guacamaya dressed up as a guacamaya
clucked a speech about flying flying about
and the assemblage of feathers celebrated till it rose in flight
and admired the guacamaya dressed up as a guacamaya

it was the day of the guacamayas

postcard

sunny yesterday today gusting wind
before the error after the hit
bang bang click click click
the cup full a while ago
at this moment it's not
nothing happened
begin to

photo

the one on the left gave
keith some cigarettes

the one next to him
with a bit of a tan
word is he got money from the mob
then burned the coca fields

the tall one the one with the mustache the grizzled one bald one
the lady he invited
and the ones dressed in gray
all of them excellent people

the one sitting down
the cynic
lights a cigar

video

in the last footage taken of the prime minister
you can see him happy toying with his whip in the aromatic breeze
off the flowering garden
his hands—open like boards—slowed the landscape's
languid movement
and his rough laughter put flocks of nightingales to flight

in the distance
on the lake's edge
spoiled crocodiles with open jaws
spurned the mutilated bodies of a few prisoners and their families

farther off
the resplendent sun

jeannie duval's cheek tickled by a paris fly 1852

in geneva i met an american ballerina
who i lived with in paris
and she taught me everything about rhythm music and
movement—said celine—

henri mahé described her thus:
huge green eyes a touch of cobalt
ever so angular like a cat's
thin elegant nose
long golden locks blushing strawberry
in curls that fell to her shoulders

any country that can produce bodies so bold in their grace
their spiritual elation so enticing
should have had much more to offer in the way of cash flow

my ballerina's hip is a lesson in patriotism

her groans
vowels: that she emits with rasping grunts
consonants: that detach themselves rustling the bushes accompanied by
the wind out to the city's edge
they are longer than all the colors

but disaster came
and tears
I tried my best to comfort her
and under emotion's spell our taxi traversed all the drugstores
at random
their scales implacable they insisted she'd gained over a kilo

she ran off to buy a ticket back to new york

it's rained so much since the afternoon she left
now that i think about it
the houses along the park are still tidy as always
the trees' shadows have grown and they reach for night in the sky

an outline for the reconstruction of events

let's say it was leipzig—long after mozart—
when the carriage pulled up to the gate
and someone blew a trumpet

let's say powder was being snorted
and a woman in a massive corset and black crinoline
brandished her enormous breasts
then soaked them in wine for the dinner guests

in another room—not visible in the drawing—
six musicians (surrounded by a crowd) struck up a minuet
for the damsel who—crouching below the table—slurped a chubby man's
member

red curtains   plush pillows   birds in flight
a cigar in the diffuse slowness of the fog

though we might all hold earth between our fingers—even mozart—
let's say it was leipzig
well of desire

michel platini gives a lecture on andré breton in the parc des princes

I never had to work to understand
the lovely entertaining terrible obstinate
personality of a ball

I always knew where i was
I could measure out the size of the field in four hemispheres
I understood the idiocy of certain refs
and commentators

the smell of grass excites me

I was born making important plays
decisive ones
I'd dream of a goal more beautiful than a knot of fish

my style is natural
and now i couldn't care less

sacred scenes from the orient

i
dismayed like a cow who's just set foot on pavement for the first time

ii
in the vegetarian restaurant
we were like a pair of cows discussing
the price of milk

iii
how noble cows are
cows must be proud of being cows
they must feel important

they must ask each other anxiously
how many people they're going to feed
clothe shoe
the brushes they'll make with their horns   their hooves
the whips that will come from their hides

how many calendars they'll pose for
and the amount of crap they have to leave along the path
in order for cows to take pride in being cows

iv
easterners say that (we) westerners have cow eyes
westerners say that they have eyes like ours but backward
easterners say westerners betray our intentions with every look
and we say they don't just betray their intentions with every look but have
    a reduced repertory of looks

easterners make fun of us because they say we all look the same
because they haven't noticed their own range of light and dark

v

a cow grazes in the fields of cabezas de san juan
it looks into the distance at the greenhouses full of workers from the magreb
looks to the sky like an ox with the sun resting on its spine of clouds
looks at the olive trees needles on the mountain
and out over the whole sewing basket: cypresses orange trees birches
it looks at the towers and the electrical wires reflected in the reservoirs
and the oil tankers disappearing down the highway
it sees in black and white with shades of gray
and swings its udders between its feet
and ruminates peacefully until evening falls

vi

one day the cows went to war
and thousands of stains saddened the sky

vii

they walk single file down a narrow hall
all bound in the same direction

(before the knife
they head to the scales
showers
disinfection)

their hooves creep forward slowly
and they don't shake off the flies that circle their tails

on a cage

he doesn't have a sunny disposition
or a great view
he doesn't sing
neither his meat nor his feathers
are worth anything
but there he is
by the painting in the parlor
balancing carefully in his minuscule universe

the difference between him and me
is that he shits on newspaper
and only eats peanuts

dust highway

your tumbleweed legs exotic orgy of ascetics and folk singers in a plus-size clothing store mmh your thighs they croon such delight and your body: dear friend disposed to return to all those ray coniff albums (on vinyl): nude aromatic beaming (clear day with scattered clouds) wine's ricochet: your body: the scent that wafts through streets moon rock toxic compass fragrant streamer: cadence of a bird as it sets over sharp peaks: each hair on your body is a branch growing in the forest each pore a ship's captain beheading the traitors each fold of flesh a shriek suffocating in a scene of night: your body: a sandstorm of hydrogen cave filled with bats rapids where princes die: i ache in the distant west physical graffiti

mmmnnmmnmnwwmwn (ants)

my landladies

all three are señoritas
though the youngest is 62

they didn't ask me for references:
one said i looked
like christ

I hope the day never comes when they ask me to fix the door
the flyswatter   the showerhead

I can see it now I'm headed toward the tub wrench in hand
witness to a terrible tragedy:

a woman with raggedy skin
and sudsy hair saying:
come closer chiquito
or if you're scared of water let's go to the bedroom
just hand me that cane
later you can beat me with it

helpless (and in my mind i still need a place to go)

in this bed where the sea slept
and the ashes of alexandria were kept
and the ants stored provisions through the holocaust summer
and the most despicable sorceress wrote her prescription for exterminating
    lovesickness

in the very same bed where the maja and venus posed
where joanna the mad mourned philip the fair across seven states
where the holy spirit impregnated mary

here in the only bed trafficked by phoenicians
which served as redbeard's map
and was the prince of ishtar's magic carpet

in this very bed the first elephant gave birth in captivity
charlie parker played the saxophone and a woman at the same time for
    the last time
and—years before—jesus mulled his mount of olives speech
it's where i learn that each bed is a country that doesn't exist when you're
    not in it

suicide note

it wasn't the dart that hit the bullseye
not the poison or the butterfly on its tip

it wasn't a lucky hit
it just took a little patience   and anyway
this was an easy target

do not charge this woman with making me blow my head off
for bringing the song of her waist to my lips

do not seek revenge on her
do not get attached to me

and don't detain her in her wanton
passion when she takes her clothes off

just light the candles
turn up the music
make sure there's plenty wine and cheese

in winter
disasters require subtlety

it's windy and god whistles a frank sinatra song

she only comes when rain threatens
when the wind sweeps photographs from her bedside

she comes for a moment for some item from the dresser
then
we make love
so we can't talk
so we can't lose sight of the matter at hand

she comes on her blackest days
when her body picks a fight
when her house abandons her

it seems my hands had something to do with her sadness

they speak of deep resentment

they speak of deep resentment
of abandonment
of internal bleeding

they say that everything was a bolt of fire
that god took off running
a shawl thrown over his head

the sea was peeling
the skin off snails

but we
we don't realize what's happened
we've been dancing
and on we go a bit unbalanced

there are words extinguished on contact

lautrec made eight studies of a redhead slicing bread and cheese for his still life

what's more he caught syphilis

when a painter—name any—falls in love
he's allowed to be wrong

henri de toulouse was right
but he ran out of money
so they left
and forgot about him

but they say he wasn't too upset in the end
and that he spent it drinking

(for the cendejas girl)

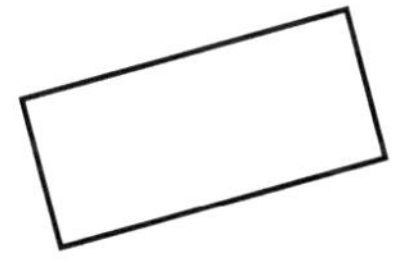

whorehouse raid

far west will never can forget

what are we
(not dust or cloud or horseshoe print)
butch cassidy sundance kid tom mix
marshal dillon the lone ranger
to the market crash
or the ubiquitous neon signs
cheerfully saddening the city

hi-ho silver

what are we billy the kid buffalo bill quick draw
the good the bad john wayne
zorro ned kelly
the corduroy heroes
to secretarial miniskirts that look at you
with the face of ursula andress

(not dust or cloud or horseshoe print)

ps:
famous cowboys is all we are
riding out the hours across the plains of your back

whorehouse raid (music by ry cooder)

while our bodies down up down
the whores ran to hide from the outlaws
and the bullets glasses shattered poker chips
playing cards on the ground
that guy who gets hit and slides down the bar
the shot to the cord that holds the chandelier
dead bodies everywhere the getaway with gun in hand and prostitute in tow
and all the beer peanuts whisky and the cash register

the cloud of dust:
the distant train whistle handkerchiefs a-wave
the slight warmth of your skin like a question
the dry branches shaking in the town's desertion

two days later the sheriff's cowardly gold star emerges
the thirsty men ready the gallows
the outlaws and whores will have crossed texas already
shit-faced and stark naked thinking about opening a cathouse in ciudad juárez
back here: the pianola has lost its poise
our bodies down up down perfect engineering
and the saloon door is swinging shut
open
shut
open

brave men don't set foot in barber shops: sue ellen

he wouldn't give his life for hers
the real story goes more like this:
everywhere they hound him
the bankers want him dead
the shopkeepers to see him hang

he's killed entire tribes
he's blown up trains
emptied out bars safes
wolves don't dare howl when he's near

some say he's aroused by the scent of lead
can smell money a mile off
eats meat raw

everyone says how they'll see him
clean-shaved and well-dressed
out for a walk on a lady's arm
on a sunday afternoon

(and the other whores cackle)

ned kelly one hot morning: norma lee

that morning he decided to raid the number three train
he cleaned the remington and the colt 45
and shoveled some hay for his horse

he jumped the bridge
a bright scarf across his face
firing shots left and right
carrying off passengers' billfolds and jewels
the safe the gold

and he searched the aisles for me—in first class obviously—
(and you must be ned kelly, i thought)
he took my arm like slamming a door and i crossed all borders
to dance with him in an oasis
where he earnestly set about tearing off my panties with his teeth

(and the whores cackle some more)

to a nose:

did you ever imagine this butch
no sundance this doesn't smell right to me

then they took my legs mounted me as many times as they wanted they filled me with beer and they sucked on my body all over the fools drank from my breasts the most sparkling elixir the most delicate alcohol in my body galloping they plowed a league the impotent canons of moaning complaint: they were useful they opened me they rode me across the plains their eyes glued to me: they scratched their names into my skin: they lassoed and domesticated every moment of my speech and away they went leaving their shirts thrown over the folding screen:

(sue ellen norma lee susan saint-john and marijane malone pretended they couldn't understand scarlett o'hara del mar's words: they didn't laugh just kept passing the bottle)

i've got gold fever 120 degrees

help: i need somebody
she's tied to the train tracks (yellow dress and white bloomers)
the cowboy hidden in the meadow watching a private show some girls
    bathing in the river
a pall mall cigarette hangs from the hero's mouth
(you can just barely make it out)

help: i need somebody
she shakes taca taca to the rhythm of the machine woo woo
she calls for help (black garters under the bloomers)
the cowboy smokes and watches/   serene
the startled river girls listen and cover their girl bits
they dissolve into mud
gaudy gallop down the mountain to rescue the damsel
backlit
at a trot cold beer from the motel what more my love
the rescue

and the railroad getting closer like a bull about to charge
and for added drama — *far west no one like ya -*
a rattlesnake looking for someone to bite

but the hero saves the damsel: and night falls
now they make love
and his horse chews contentedly in the barn
alongside a tractor   a rocking chair on the porch
an ousted dog   farther off a mail post
and the rattlesnake cooking over coals

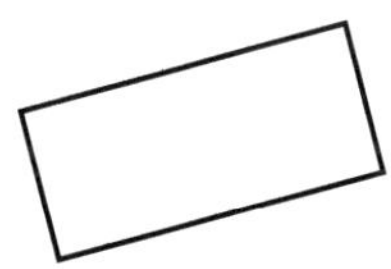

short film

suddenly new york was left without joseph brodsky

an old car goes wheezing by
a jittery dude offers you what you want
prostitutes in coats huddle together against the wind
a bunch of suits stagger plastered out of a bar
a bum reaches out his hand
at the end of the road lights flash
as a patrol car makes a slow right
a couple comes out of a theater
two black guys talk
and in the shop window across the way
a pair of silk stockings
hang silently
more seemingly indispensable than we

blue medley

he met her in a bar or at a concert
and he talked about how you have to be careful with bonsais
or some other fad he'd read about in the melody mirror

he probably doesn't remember if he asked her name
or just forgot it
but he runs his hands over her ass
and they dance

she moans
pieces of clothing fall to the floor

he died a few months later
and the incident caught the attention of various papers
they wrote his biography (several times)
they paid tribute
the president never got tired of talking about him

how to picture him going over that cliff in his yellow volkswagen
now when he's in the kitchen in his socks
looking for whisky or some rum
if there's any still left

he could probably learn to love her if she doused her body with bourbon

she's just run a towel between her legs
because she's been beneath a middle-aged guy
who had to be forced to use a condom
and she danced for him and sucked his cock
for the 100 dollars they'd agreed on
at the corner of sunset and western

now she adjusts her pantyhose and leather skirt
puts on her shoes
zips her black jacket halfway up her bust
shakes out her hair
says goodbye with a big smile before closing the door
and walks out into the relentless drizzle
alone and lit by streetlights

she drags her purse languidly
and there's something poetic about it all

no detective movie

no detective movie is successful
if it doesn't show the outline of a fan
spinning on the detective's desk

what would love be without a woman leaving her shadow beneath a streetlight

it's the shadow that interests the shark
how to say tree without mentioning the shadow

the shadow is a dark mannequin
it's the concept closest to god

it's keeping quiet and knowing all

the wife's description of a paul klee painting

it's got character: he's thrown a bunch of vases against the wall

it's elegant: he's broken dishes and smashed spoons forks porcelain figurines a tape recorder and ashtrays against the floor to create a harmonious landscape

it's in good taste: he arsenicly interwove a dialect reminiscent of chinese horoscopes

and she's angry because there's dust on the books
and she's blondeasy-going
and never turns down a martini

epilogue

mick jagger won't sing satisfaction at 50

you were in your mother's arms
and the country in díaz ordaz's

the black panther made wembley go wild
the crystal ball in his cleats
the field: imperial carpet rolled out: but no

bobby moore—so serious—
charlton the little bourgeois boy who greased the ball with melancholy
& gordon banks reversing gravity
(between nail-biting video takes)
they came close to the jules rimet
with a phantom goal that everyone saw didn't go in
and let the jules rimet be kissed by royalty
yes isabel ii the one they threw a bottle at her car
in belfast

and franco: spain full of dust and grey streets
johnson bombing hai phong hanoi
and new delhi sanctioning the slaughter of sacred cows

marlon brando films mutiny on the bounty
and for 200 000 dollars he buys
tetiaroa island in tahiti from madame duran
with the promise (very hippie of him) not to cut down a single tow tree
and then tragedies: the beatles refuse to give concerts
paul mccartney erases ringo's tracks and rerecords with a different drummer
yoko ono sets in motion her evil plan to destroy the foursome

you were gurgling and people were talking about the death of george duhamel
buster keaton anna akhmatova andré breton
about the red guard in peking
about fidel castro and the encyclical of paul xi
about polypropylene
or peter paul & mary

: and the whole world was very busy
me for example
I was devoting myself to commentary on all matters
regarding brigitte bardot's ass

galaxy limited café

sex in space and everything in between

the incredible world of machines

—what do you want for your birthday
—a terminator
—what is that and where can i buy it
—the internet

314 dollars and a few days later it arrived at the house
excitedly she tore open the box
a hair-raising plastic device hot vibrating skin colored
with accessories for penetrating vagina and anus at the same time
with three different speeds and ultra-toxic batteries

working those controls
will make you think about the big questions

her pupils trembled in her eyes
squeezing her hands into fists she drooled
and screamed like she'd been dosed with napalm

within a few days i got the hang of it
monday terminator
tuesday terminator ii judgement day
wednesday terminator iii rise of the machines
thursday terminator iv salvation
until little by little i turned into another of the toy's accessories

the incredible world of machines

let's see if the terminator leaves her sweet messages
or refills her wine glass
or gazes at her from the other side of the room

let's see

she's already telling me she wants the alien
an adorable space bauble that runs on solar energy
and makes you feel like your stomach is bursting open

july 27 1896:

dallas newsly publishes the first mention of the ufo's presence
skeptics establish that the aforementioned is a sign
of the planet's imminent demise

and at least there could have been a law
or a political editorial to condemn the event
the report breaking centuries of silence

our ancestors' fascination with the topic passed
and so did thousands of years and lights before we saw those initials in alignment
that confirmed the ufo existed even without existing

galaxy limited cafe

july 27 2003:

: just a few months ago
we couldn't imagine suppressing the horror of the red hostility of mars
and its inhabitants:
wretched devoted ambitious genies who wanted to put an end to us
and our water and our plutonium and our architecture
but our heroes with their dodges chokeholds and theme songs
have kept us unharmed
unharmed in some films

nasa predicted that the probability of life existing on mars was
1 in 10 000 000
but the *mars space orbit* (official mouthpiece of nasa itself in all matters
    martian)
confirmed that on that planet of carmine deserts
there are tunnels like tentacles
which with a dynamic frequency enter and exit the surface carrying gases
    and liquids
: these circumstances raise the suspicion that mars in all its rotundity
might itself be an intelligent being
: a cosmic medusa

there was a time when the milky way was a ribbon of lactose
and gods shone in the cosmos (lost in space:
danger danger danger danger)
and the galaxy was vast
and we were ever closer

now
incandescent mars watches us suspended in the dawn
like a genie with its arms crossed
and no one does a thing

july 27 1967: (those words would make any sailor blush)

across the grazing animal's spine
where the sun scatters the first symptoms of its yellow fever
pick-ups packed with marijuana head down the mountain toward the border
between gun fights and women who keep walking unfazed
(helicopters arrowheads in the sky carry dust
worth 7 000 sheep 3 000 camels 500 yokes of oxen 500 donkeys and livestock
  crawling like ants over the earth)
when the world was a hint of brush in vast desert sands
the extraterrestrials had already arrived
when the world was believed to be a clay tower
that reached almost to the clouds
or a flat surface held up on three legs like a table
or a great sound spinning in the gramophone of the cosmos
the extraterrestrials were here making pyramids
and gardens and waterfalls and invisible books and molecules of wolfram
and horror movies (still censored)
and several nude beaches
and they didn't rest
when it was believed that the world was a species going extinct
and that we didn't exist
or that a muscled man carried the world on his back
or that a magnetic accident had set it spinning
or that it was an aquiferous eclosion fragmented at different temperatures
or a telescope's distance or a bar code
the extraterrestrials were here sculpting stones
pots tombs and inventing blackmail

they'd already sown coveted herbs and aphrodisiacs
and made landing strips and false documents and huge bribes
and before they left and we arrived
they'd already had the rest of the landscape all packed up
leaving those gaps
where the pick-up trucks (and helicopters) deliver their merchandise right
on time

czeslaw milosz gets off the train at fuengirola

what do i have in common with your prairies
where the taciturn beasts chewed grass before the flood
never lifting their heads

there was nothing on earth that i wanted
as if i existed only for the perishing of land and men

there is no witchcraft in my words
I speak silent as a cloud
or tree

I am part of a system of polarized multicolored crystal spheres
that furl and unfurl the thread of phosphorescent liquids
held in place thanks to gravity
and the combustion of certain gases

I know that the ocean unleashed its tired tongues at the edge of the sea
and the lighthouse is lit
for me   for the shore
each in turn

i'll be part of it (brunch remasterized)

frank sings the same songs and always the same way
orange juice to wake up
he doesn't catch the news doesn't know about the top ten doesn't answer the phone
he spends his afternoons on the treadmill looking at a poster of malibu
secretary days off ballerinas musicians private priest
murmurs of the mafia float like the roar of the sea
cat claw guarana sealskin tai chi black jack
but frank's wife is calm as water in a pool
she controls the heat domestic staff jewelry box
she wears a robe and mask to sleep
for years she's been calling a restaurant to order roast beef
and in spite of her daughter getting drunk and stripping every time there's a party
and swallowing as many pills as she could
nothing happens
nothing will happen
frank sings the same songs and always the same way

no altoids or white house or blue dress no hillary no clitoris lodged in anyone's campaign trail

on the soundtrack charly watts' drums
sound just like the typewriter of a reporter from the most purulent small
    town rag
elastic whiplash 36 b (gas gas gas)
without her life is x
—I think when she changes position—
: light speaks   rocks breathe
like the statues
who before being statues were a pile of deformed rocks
and other ones rose up just to make a wall
and she thinks
that aliens came here with everything we need for life: pollution   war
    the faintest idea
the word and the beginning
when the constellations draw everything invented
and charly watts' drums (holes and crispy bread)
find what they're looking for

alamo blues (death penalty)

here the matter ends smoking in an uncomfortable chair
150 000 watts away from foxtrot
for sure:
the band plays so quiet they can hear our conversation
and the other tables' too
the drumsticks like water
nothing to do with crickets a night of insomnia
they play something that sounds like satchmo and might not be
the waitress chews gum like a hussy and might not be
: the elevator door is fake   the pianist's dentures fake
fake hair   fake bell sounds from the cash register
and some beer is non-alcoholic
and all that works
: most people are more afraid of cigarettes than they are of congress :
fresh packs excite me
breaking the cellophane with the gold tape like the ribbon on a gift
the cigarettes' embers are street lamps lighting up the travelers
: but here they only allow the harmless blue smoke
of bombers on the plains
that make their way through the mountains searching for ashtrays in the sky
and heroes will live forever
while texaco signs throb dying on the highway
and jazz goes on playing softly in the background

banner flag

in 1800-something a huge apple pie called america sat cooling on a windowsill
they came from everywhere to get a slice
: the coal companies used the bones of 2 500 000 buffalos to bring the oven up to temp
and a brown cloud cooked in the forest

america is a brilliant sun reflecting off the mississippi
a casino in the middle of the desert
a barrel floating down a waterfall's vertebrae
a snow-capped mountain in ochre light like a glass of bourbon in the vertigo of the peak
on its cliffs the mustangs neigh behind the mavericks' charge
and in their echo you can make out the geometry of the falcon and other species that emigrated
leaving thousands of beautiful oil rigs to gush from the hard clay

in 1800-something the world was a torture chamber
opium war and the sale of hong kong
a king was losing his head
a bassoon and a harpsichord winding down a sonata
baudelaire and vavasseur searching for a bed on the cobblestones
and the people squealing like newborn rats suckling at typhus syphilis and tuberculosis

america was a dragging of chains in rhythm and blues
steamship   miner's helmet virginia tobacco sending up signals
the wind covering the plains with a smallpox-infected blanket
one boot stepping on the moon and the other on the necks of black slaves
    in the cotton fields
and all that came to pass: mardi gras beads
asphalt pastures mercury lamp reeds   fruit-bearing skyscrapers:
today they remain jingling with electrical failures
and the delirious fever of chemical horror

ballad of the last bombs

ron is an old black and white movie actor
who made money with anyone he could selling interviews and guns
meanwhile
various bombs fell on the world
as for george
he's an oil rancher who drove a huge pickup with a longhorn on the front
next to his wife gnawing a corn cob and spitting bits of kernel out the window
and more bombs fell on the world
bill on the other hand
smoked marijuana and loved his friends to suck him off
that didn't stop more and more bombs from falling
but different was the era of georgy—george's son—
who fervidly sought his father's affection
amidst the bombs falling on the world

from california to des moines hitching "un raid" to chicago

he was a black man in the days when the only thing harder was being a
black woman
and he was photographed only twice

he was a black man: the son of slaves:
and he was a layabout who never wanted to move his hands
except to hold a harmonica
which he blew with a train in his lungs

his final years were spent with semen fanatics
his mother taught him how to dress elegantly
and when he reached the intersection of highways 61 and 49
he ran into that girl
: he'd always thought he only liked black women
together they howl quiver making perfect circles
(but he'd always let his guitar play alone)
and this busty little redhead apple faced fruitcake freckles
sucked him off with such tenderness
it was as if the oppressing races across all of history
were begging humanity's forgiveness
for having ever been racist

after that night
the black man began to play those shrill chords
that seem like they'll shatter every window in the city
and slip the elastic of shoulder blades
: those were nights of pool triangle cannon shots money on the felt
and the black man slipping a slide
like the whole world falling into the corner pocket

: he was arrested on charges of being black
and carrying a guitar
the police beat the hell out of him
so then he had the right to a phone call
and he called don: a famous producer
who came to get him out on 33 dollar bail
and drove him to a motel
he gave him a bottle of whisky   a burrito
and 45 cents for breakfast
: that way early tomorrow we can record a fine 78
don suggested

but when he got home the telephone rang desperately
he picked it up and it was the black man again
—what now? (don asked nervously)
—I'm alone so alone so so alone so alone: i learned everything i know in a cemetery
—I don't understand
—there's no one more alone than me not the stars on the flag not the stains on the moon
and there's a lady here with me
and she's inclined to stay the night and ease my pain
for 50 cents
but I'm short 5

he was a black man in the days when the only thing harder was being a black woman
and he was photographed only twice

his guitar played in both mississippi's ears at the very same time
he should have written better songs more of them
but he didn't have time
the notes of his life were tired ones
and when he was nearsighted looking for his glasses
someone gave him a bottle of whisky
(his new lover's husband, it seems)
the stage lights shone bright
he took a long drink
and played one last time

how to get to montego bay (the movie)

the porn actress's mother proudly played her daughter's movies
to show all the neighbors what a big deal she was
(there are a lot of faces out there
that only wish they could get covered with semen by the last sailor
in the shipwreck of humanity)
her mother would grin at each orgasm
then she'd tense and suffer
when her daughter took it up the ass
: it's like life itself—she'd muse—
another person's pleasure is always a turn-on :
and her daughter howling like a train
that wants to leave the station
while the crowd's still climbing aboard

team mascot

a beautiful specimen—better fed than idi amin's—
slinking under water lashing the colors of the fake swamp
: a million visitors in just a few days
the most recent was last night when they tossed in a chicken thigh on a
    fishing line
and it bit
the hook came out through its nose
tying together its mandibles
they kidnapped it
the whole neighborhood gathered
they knifed it and kicked it and stoned it and beat it with brooms
they snuffed it out with skillets and hammers but the radio kept on playing
when its foot came off
in chunks they threw it into stew pots
: soup's the only thing you can make from the tail
but no one passed up the nails   skin
or the gummy moss broth brought out by cooktops
the next day
plastered all over the city walls
were posters announcing
a crocodile has escaped from the zoo and should be considered very dangerous

ray tom's daring heroes: vidal sassoon gloria vanderbil sergio valente foretell the name jordache (op cit levi strauss & co)

I was against the chemical permutation that breaks the body down
and inevitably carries it into death
like the grenades of fragmentation
on pay per view
I am a seal on a glacier waiting for the club

I go out to watch the afternoon die wearing a scarf
that flutters like a bend in the road
where there are clouds that move the way you move
(clouds that love me)
and look like semen against your lips

: everything is music while the music lasts
and the silence—which is never heard—
dies with a little noise

I'm up against the wall
(I don't want to hear the screaming flames the hum of the guns)
: the wind will hurl itself into the void
the moon will hang itself on the horizon

studies among the crowd

you've been stone
juice
thousands of ducks flying into my eyes
I throb designed for fun
the orchestra of your skeleton watched me from afar
and i was learning to appreciate the virtues of cats
(I'm a regular modern guy
who likes a good blow job
and dreams of finding a suitcase with a million dollars
: with or without my cock inside you I've always been yours)
it's the belch   the tic
dry leaves blowing around on the pavement
just like soldiers in a trench
(you've got to think about everything
to be here)
fingernails neck napes dysmenorrhoea trichomoniasis
belly button lint
your body is a siren
a trombone on the car radio banging against my pancreas
a city retreating along a river
gleaming faintly

fat sums for thin credibility

hot we holler in the middle of the desert sharing a smoke hand in hand
we're the biggest idiots for the idiots in charge
a raid   evidence
a racetrack with the highest stakes
: acid
a guitar solo long and intense that everyone hums along to
our wheat paste fixes the present in a dotted line to the past
making an origami shriek
because between us
crack pioneers the web binary code
changing up our "look"
or our copilots in a shiny convertible putting an arm around us
or in a line deep in your nostrils
we are a flower in the window
a steam bath outside the bus terminal
a steaming plate coming out of the microwave
and we walk amid the dust of the sky
like a sophisticated modern machine
that has always been obsolete

god lives across the street from me

in a big house
with a huge garden where all his cats live

the gardener over at god's house is a muscular dude
who works with his shirt off

and once in a while we spot god in socks
listening to music in his garage

or hugging a young woman the way god does
and she hugs him back the only way you can really hug god

god watches the cats chase after love
and cockroaches

with a wave of his hand he waters the plants closes the door
reviews his correspondence or uncorks a dusty bottle

it went on like this every day until one day and suddenly
he disappeared

an ambulance outside the house
seemed to clear things up a bit

but no
he'd just gone and disappeared

maybe the cats had told him: get out of here you've never done anyone
    any good
or maybe while he napped the cockroaches ate him up

lullaby

I don’t remember how i detached myself windy from liquid to gas
or how i saw the developing stains
what could i have known of geometry after a couple hours in the game
hearing nothing but voices: or rather dolphins
a resonant howling that always accompanies me
(john cage discovered that the humming in his ears
was the sound of his blood moving

judith was a little girl and she believed that hum was god talking to her
and despaired because she couldn’t make out the words)
and right now it’s loud and clear

I remember how smiling was a good response
and that the rooftop peak is a permanent doubt

and that i was there
understanding something
and trying to forget everything

eureka: six knots on the james river

when his girlfriend broke a glass she bled while singing
he began to write and run around to bars
where they'd serve him a glass of all the other customers' dregs
but the night selma danced with a boa
in front of a famous editor
who stuck tips in her waistband
he agreed to look at the manuscript
swearing that no scientific achievement to date
could touch the importance of this work
(the year was 1847:
electricity existed in lab sketches
the lightbulb was just months from being invented
those were the days when the atom was indivisible)
and it refuted the astronomers
asserting that *some of our galaxy's nebulas*
were other galaxies outside of our galaxy
which foretold
a progressive dwindling of the speed of elements in the face of gravity
and the ultimate cessation of expansion
which would lead to star collapse
a superparticle
where the galaxy would be absorbed by another unity
the editor nodded
selma still undressed with whisky on her nipples
the boa drawing a spiral with its tongue
and two antennas in the penumbra of the cries
the editor traded three cents for the manuscript
and after a while he left without seeing anyone
a few days later the manuscript was a book in shop windows:
eight cents a copy

(but it didn't attract the slightest interest)
in spite of the fact that he would—constantly—recite passages
at salons and in public
drawing small crowds and huge laughs
while the police
bored
waited for the orderlies to arrive

climax with double cheese:
exterior somewhere in the world
a subtitle appears

beneath the raging storm
in a condo on the mountainside
furnished with a white sofa and coffee table
without lights or water and dimly lit by candles and battery-powered lamps
a super hot chick paces desperately back and forth
talking insistently into her cell phone
she wears an aqua g-string a see-through robe that exposes her gorgeous
expertly augmented breasts
she's frustrated: biting her lips and chewing her nails
pressing the buttons of her telephone

outside: the rain pounds and bounces on the cement
taking in the sound of the earth (pan to the window)
lightning bolts illuminate the trees as they're tossed about in the gusting wind
and thunder booms (surround sound)
and even louder we hear a knock at the door

knock knock

the hot chick opens it with a towel in hand on the other side of the door a soaking wet young man appears dressed as a pizza delivery boy: he wears a nextel clipped to his belt and he straddles a motorbike and in his right hand he holds aloft a special with pepperoni mozzarella and peppers

– pizza horny señora (the kid doesn't seem surprised to see the gorgeous expertly augmented breasts or aqua g-string or bitten nails or vibrating cell phone of the hot chick who asks with a doubtful look:)

- how much it is?
- one hundred seventy-five fifty – the kid answers instantly
- okay i need to go get the money: come on in and make yourself comfortable you can dry off with this towel (she gives him the towel) and drink the martini that's already waiting on the coffee table don't ask me why i made two (close-up of the martinis on the table)

right at that moment, the voice of the manager from pizza horny comes blaring through the nextel speaker:

- alert alert: high alert: this is the manager of pizza horny: the hurricane has hit the city and we are suspending all activities: high alert i need all delivery personnel not to return to base because it's flooded and the wind carried off the front awning and the chalkboard with our specials and the mascot dude: alert high alert

the only sound is the rain
and the hot chick with the aqua g-string and the see-through robe that exposes her gorgeous expertly augmented breasts presses play on her ipod (and out comes smooth boring trivial music)
the pizza boy is naked with a mild erection the martini in his hand and the olive in his mouth

- what do you do when you're not delivering pizza
- I study library science
- oh
- yes: I'm in my fourth semester
- I've heard that library scientists are known for being really big
- no: you're thinking of middle managers
- then it seems like you chose the wrong specialty
- no: everyone in my family is in management and i got their good genes

as soon as she hears these words she starts to blow him
she sucks comfortably
she closes her eyes
it seems like that manager's cock on a library scientist's body has always been right there
going in and out like a cub in its den (or something gentler)
the pizza boy is awkward
but his nonexistent prowess is good enough to rip off the hot chick's g-string
and even get down on his knees
stick out his tongue and park it between her clitoris and urethra which he caresses with circular motions (close-up of her urethra)

the music plays between moans
(the camera pans to the window)
the storm is devastating
raindrops fall on the ground in watery circles
and other drops fall in those circles
forming other watery circles inside the circles
there's lighting
thunder
the hillside is crumbling: huge rocks seal off the roads and crash down onto homes down below: the river bursts its banks and the city starts to flood

suddenly the pizza delivery boy sits up
flips the hot chick around and does her doggie-style for 20 minutes
her gorgeous expertly augmented breasts
swinging back and forth rhythmically

at minute 21 the pizza delivery boy's nextel speaker crackles with the voice of another pizza delivery boy who's trapped in the french quarter calling for help:

– help help can anyone hear me I'm trapped in the french quarter: my motorbike's distributor got wet and i can't get it to start please help me: the hilltop collapses: there are cars floating across the asphalt: the hot chick with gorgeous augmented breasts doesn't understand what's going on and the pizza delivery boy explains:

– he's really close by we should help him: he could get run over

she doesn't show the slightest interest but the pizza delivery boy grabs the nextel

– come over here, buddy: I'm with a really nice generous family that's helping me out

traveling shot of the city:
the roadways submerged under the rain
water rises out of the sewers and the drainpipes are clogged with bags cans bottles diapers toilet paper shoes auto parts television antennas neon signs:
(zoom out)
in the background: in its fury the river current dislodges the bridge supports and restraining walls around the avenues:
cars tumble into the tide:
in the foreground: a pair of trembling frightened birds huddle under the sodden branch of a violently shaking tree:

now a low camera angle and we see on the white sofa the pizza delivery boy sucking the clitoris of the hot chick with gorgeous augmented breasts and in the next shot
she looks straight into the camera and between incoherent noises she stammers so good yes yes mmmm when abruptly the pizza guy's coworker walks in a boy just like the first one but a little taller with a big nose and he's got two muddy boxes of wet pizza that he couldn't deliver: a hawaiian and the classic crunchy vegetarian

– sorry i didn't mean to interrupt (he turns around and opens the door):

(shot from the open door) the sound of the rain is deafening: a psychotic hammer: a giant pool of water threatens to climb the last few inches and pour into the house: the pizza guy's coworker closes the door and anxiously turns back prey to unprecedented fear

– welcome (whispers the hot chick with gorgeous augmented breasts as she opens her legs and licks the index finger of her left hand and adds:)
I don't usually like pizza delivery boys unless they're handsome hot and dirty

(wide shot) the flash of a lightning bolt comes through the window and illuminates the hot chick's gorgeous expertly augmented breasts: her aureolas are the size of gerber lids: and at that instant we hear the crash of thunder the pizza delivery boy's coworker lets his pants fall around his ankles and his dick springs to attention

– wow you've got a big one – exclaims the hot chick with gorgeous augmented breasts
– yeah: i study management – the coworker replies proudly
– he's just so shy – the pizza delivery boy says apologetically

the hot chick with gorgeous expertly augmented breasts takes hold of both dicks like they're drum sticks and taps out a good syncopated beat like she's playing a snare and she tells the pizza delivery boy

– guys with big ones get more respect

cut

(a shot of the white sofa) the pizza delivery boy is seated and his eyes are glazed over like he's in a trance he drools slightly
the hot chick with gorgeous augmented breasts straddles him

riding jauntily along a mountain of winding groans
and at the same time she's fucked by the pizza delivery boy's coworker:
the guys moan a little but she howls like a gleeful dog greeting the dawn

(close-up on the hot chick's ass and the pizza delivery boy's coworker's dick entering it) though we hear thunder it's evident that the hot chick with expertly augmented breasts has an ass full of farts: the mix of noises lends a profundity to the muzak coming from the ipod and with every thrust gases slip out some of them thick and others airy or faster or happy little sweet nothings and a great number of dirty murmurs that end with a long gush from the hole:

the pizza delivery boy's coworker closes his eyes and breathes deeply: (close-up of his nose his nostrils flaring) his sweaty evocative face: (a slow fade)

cut to (close-up of the pizza delivery boy's coworker's face with his nostrils flaring and his eyes blindfolded cut to an open shot of a room full of flatulent women facing him):

the diversity of sounds is overwhelming damp abrupt dry childish rattling shrill roaring husky trumpeting and he: focusing his sense of smell he recognizes in the farthest corner of the room some soft fragrant farts that arc through the air agile as tigers through a ring of fire these are the farts of the hot chick with gorgeous expertly augmented breast: (dissolve)

cut to (close-up on the face of the pizza delivery boy's coworker he breathes deeply and opens his eyes suddenly on hearing the wall splitting open and the aggressive insertion of water into the house: the camera shakes):

the door cannot hold it breaks gives way to an entire ocean:
the ipod dies instantly: the lamps go out:
the house is plunged into cacophonous darkness:

the white sofa with its lustful trio floats in the middle of the room amid
desolate slices of pizza
:the action is frenetic pumping blow jobs maximum speed fucking
the hot chick with gorgeous expertly augmented breasts squirts and raises
the level of the water inside the house
the window shatters:

the deluge uproots the flowers in the park
ruins houses and rips out support beams molding metal tools woodwork tiles
glass shards:
and the threesome stuck together at the genitals on a white sofa float out of
the house
and follow the course of the river through the neighborhood
beneath the rain to the rhythm of the sea and the rapids and the mud and
the landslides that also drag along rocks tires syringes motorcycles tread-
mills glasses of dry ice wrappers handguns home appliances stuffed deer
heads pick-ups with bullet-proof glass and the camera which (underwater
shot) zooms in:
a van submerged underneath an overpass
a woman and little girl
desperately waving their arms from inside:

the rain smacks against the body of the hot chick with gorgeous expertly
augmented breasts like bullets and she has an orgasm
causing the city's sculptures to collapse and the camera to stumble

the sofa floats away:
the pizza delivery boy and the pizza delivery boy's coworker taking turns
ejaculating in the mouth of the hot chick with gorgeous expertly augment-
ed breasts
and then ejaculating again in her mouth and ejaculating again and ejacu-
lating again and ejaculating again
and the hot chick with gorgeous expertly augmented breasts

holds her breath
smiles with a viscous and inanimate shine on her lips
and fixes her gaze on nothingness:

the white sofa – a mint chiclet – rushes toward the river
the bodies come apart and are thrown off flying
they spin in the gyre
of a city-sized toilet bowl

about the author & translator

—José Eugenio Sánchez (Guadalajara, México 1965) is the author of *jack boner & the rebellion* (Almadía, 2014), *suite prelude: a/h1n1* (Toad Press, 2011), *galaxy limited café* (Almadía, 2011), *escenas sagradas del oriente* (Almadía, 2009), *la felicidad es una pistola caliente* (Colección Visor de Poesía, España, 2004), and *physical graffiti* (Colección Visor de Poesía, España, 1998). He is a member of FONCA's Sistema Nacional de Creadores de Arte. In 2006, he was invited by the U.S. State Department to participate in the University of Iowa's International Writing Program, receiving an Honorary Fellow Writer grant. He won the Loewe Foundation's 10th International Prize for Young Poets. In 2014, he curated the Festival de Poesía en Voz Alta at the Casa del Lago at UNAM. Currently, he performs with his poetry and rock band, Un País Cayendo a Pedazos. Their album, *por ahí no es amor* (sonido sexofónico), was released in 2016.

—Anna Rosenwong is a translator, editor, poet, and educator. She won the Best Translated Book Award for Rocio Ceron's *Diorama*, and has received fellowships from the National Endowment for the Arts, the Banff International Literary Translation Centre, the University of Iowa, and the American Literary Translators Association. She is the translation editor of *Anomaly*. Her scholarly and creative work has been featured in such venues as *World Literature Today, The Kenyon Review, Gulf Coast, Translation Studies, Asymptote, Two Lines, Words Without Borders, Jacket2,* and *Modern Poetry Today*. Chapbooks include *suite prelude a/h1n1* and *climax with double cheese* (José Eugenio Sánchez), *AND THE OWNERS OF THE WORLD NO LONGER FEAR US* (Victoria Guerrero Peirano), and *By Way of Explanation* (Anna Guercio Rosenwong). She holds an MFA from the University of Iowa and a Ph.D. from the University of California, Irvine. More at annarosenwong.com.